Contents

	page
Away in a manger	4
Hark! The herald angels sing	6
The first Nowell	8
O come all ye faithful	10
Once in royal David's city	13
O little town of Bethlehem	15
While shepherds watched their flocks by night	18
The three kings	20
The holly and the ivy	22
Winter's snow	24
Christians, awake	26
God rest you merry gentlemen	28
Good King Wenceslas	31
Good Christian men rejoice	34
Silent night	36
Unto us a child is born	37
I saw three ships	38
Ding dong! merrily on high	41
As with gladness men of old	42

Published by Ladybird Books Ltd
27 Wrights Lane London W8 5TZ
A Penguin Company
3 5 7 9 10 8 6 4 2

Printed in Italy

Well Loved
CAROLS

chosen by AUDREY DALY
illustrated by PETER CHURCH

Ladybird

Away in a manger

Away in a manger, no crib for a bed,
The little Lord Jesus laid down his
    sweet head.
The stars in the bright sky looked down
    where he lay,
The little Lord Jesus asleep on the hay.

The cattle are lowing, the baby awakes,
But little Lord Jesus no crying he makes.
I love thee, Lord Jesus! Look down from
    the sky,
And stay by my bedside till morning is nigh.

Be near me, Lord Jesus; I ask thee to stay
Close by me for ever, and love me, I pray.
Bless all the dear children in thy tender care,
And fit us for heaven, to live with thee there.

Hark! The herald angels sing

Hark! The herald angels sing
Glory to the new-born King;
Peace on Earth and mercy mild,
God and sinners reconciled:
Joyful all ye nations rise,
Join the triumph of the skies,
With the angelic host proclaim,
Christ is born in Bethlehem.
> *Hark! The herald angels sing*
> *Glory to the new-born King.*

Christ, by highest heaven adored,
Christ, the everlasting Lord,
Late in time behold him come
Offspring of the Virgin's womb;
Veiled in flesh the Godhead see;
Hail the incarnate Deity!
Pleased as man with man to dwell,
Jesus, our Emmanuel.

Hail the heaven-born Prince of Peace!
Hail the Sun of Righteousness!
Light and life to all he brings,
Risen with healing in his wings;
Mild he lays his glory by,
Born that man no more may die,
Born to raise the sons of Earth,
Born to give them second birth.

The first Nowell

The first Nowell the angel did say
Was to certain poor shepherds in fields as
   they lay:
In fields where they lay keeping their sheep
On a cold winter's night that was so deep.
   Nowell, Nowell, Nowell, Nowell,
   Born is the King of Israel.

They looked up and saw a star,
Shining in the east, beyond them far,
And to the Earth it gave great light,
And so it continued both day and night.

And by the light of that same star,
Three wise men came from country far;
To seek for a King was their intent,
And to follow the star wherever it went.

This star drew nigh to the north-west,
O'er Bethlehem it took its rest,
And there it did both stop and stay
Right over the place where Jesus lay.

Then entered in those wise men three,
Full reverently upon their knee,
And offered there in his presence
Their gold and myrrh and frankincense.

Then let us all with one accord
Sing praises to our Heavenly Lord,
That hath made heaven and Earth of nought,
And with His blood mankind hath bought.

O come all ye faithful

O come, all ye faithful,
Joyful and triumphant,
O come ye, O come ye to Bethlehem;
Come and behold him,
Born the King of angels:

O come, let us adore him,
O come, let us adore him,
O come, let us adore him,
  Christ the Lord!

God of God,
Light of Light,
Lo, he abhors not the Virgin's womb;
Very God,
Begotten, not created.

See how the shepherds,
Summoned to his cradle,
Leaving their flocks, draw nigh with lowly fear;
We too will thither
Bend our joyful footsteps.

Sing, choirs of angels,
Sing in exultation,
Sing, all ye citizens of heaven above;
Glory to God
In the highest.

Yea, Lord, we greet thee,
Born this happy morning,
Jesu, to thee be glory given;
Word of the Father,
Now in flesh appearing.

Once in royal David's city

Once in royal David's city
Stood a lowly cattle shed,
Where a mother laid her baby
In a manger for his bed:
Mary was that mother mild,
Jesus Christ her little child.

He came down to Earth from heaven,
Who is God and Lord of all,
And his shelter was a stable,
And his cradle was a stall;
With the poor, and mean, and lowly,
Lived on Earth our Saviour holy.

And through all his wondrous childhood
He would honour and obey,
Love and watch the lowly maiden,
In whose gentle arms he lay:
Christian children all must be
Mild, obedient, good as he.

For he is our childhood's pattern:
Day by day like us he grew,
He was little, weak, and helpless,
Tears and smiles like us he knew;
And he feeleth for our sadness,
And he shareth in our gladness.

Not in that poor lowly stable,
With the oxen standing by,
We shall see him, but in heaven
Set at God's right hand on high.
When, like stars, his children crowned
All in white shall wait around.

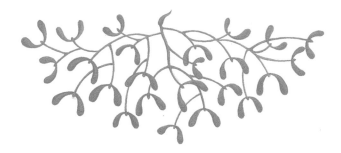

O little town of Bethlehem

O little town of Bethlehem,
How still we see thee lie!
Above thy deep and dreamless sleep
The silent stars go by.
Yet in thy dark streets shineth
The everlasting light;
The hopes and fears of all the years
Are met in thee tonight.

O morning stars, together
Proclaim the holy birth,
And praises sing to God the King,
And peace to men on Earth;
For Christ is born of Mary;
And, gathered all above,
While mortals sleep, the angels keep
Their watch of wondering love.

How silently, how silently,
The wondrous gift is given!
So God imparts to human hearts
The blessings of his heaven.
No ear may hear his coming;
But in this world of sin,
Where meek souls will receive him, still
The dear Christ enters in.

O holy Child of Bethlehem,
Descend to us, we pray;
Cast out our sin, and enter in,
Be born in us today.
We hear the Christmas angels
The great glad tidings tell:
O come to us, abide with us,
Our Lord Emmanuel.

While shepherds watched their flocks by night

While shepherds watched their flocks
   by night,
All seated on the ground,
The angel of the Lord came down,
And glory shone around.

'Fear not,' said he (for mighty dread
   Had seized their troubled mind);
'Glad tidings of great joy I bring
To you and all mankind.

'To you in David's town this day
Is born of David's line
A saviour, who is Christ the Lord;
And this shall be the sign:

'The heavenly babe you there shall find
To human view displayed,
All meanly wrapped in swathing bands,
And in a manger laid.'

Thus spake the seraph: and forthwith
Appeared a shining throng
Of angels praising God, who thus
Addressed their joyful song:

'All glory be to God on high,
And to the Earth be peace;
Goodwill henceforth from heaven to men
Begin and never cease.'

19

We three kings

We three kings of Orient are,
Bearing gifts we traverse afar
Field and fountain, moor and mountain,
Following yonder star:

> *O star of wonder, star of night,*
> *Star with royal beauty bright,*
> *Westward leading, still proceeding,*
> *Guide us to thy perfect light.*

Born a king on Bethlehem plain,
Gold I bring, to crown him again
King forever, ceasing never,
Over us all to reign.

Frankincense to offer have I;
Incense owns a deity nigh:
Prayer and praising, all men raising,
Worship him, God most high.

Myrrh is mine; its bitter perfume
Breathes a life of gathering gloom;
Sorrowing, sighing, bleeding, dying,
Sealed in the stone cold tomb.

Glorious now, behold him arise,
King, and God, and sacrifice!
Heaven sings alleluya,
Alleluya the Earth replies.

The holly and the ivy

The holly and the ivy,
When they are both full grown,
Of all the trees that are in the wood,
The holly bears the crown.

> *O, the rising of the sun*
> *And the running of the deer,*
> *The playing of the merry organ,*
> *Sweet singing in the choir.*

The holly bears a blossom,
As white as the lily flower,
And Mary bore sweet Jesus Christ,
To be our sweet Saviour.

The holly bears a berry,
As red as any blood,
And Mary bore sweet Jesus Christ,
To do poor sinners good.

The holly bears a prickle,
As sharp as any thorn,
And Mary bore sweet Jesus Christ
On Christmas Day in the morn.

The holly bears a bark,
As bitter as any gall,
And Mary bore sweet Jesus Christ
For to redeem us all.

Winter's snow

See amid the winter's snow,
Born for us on Earth below;
See the tender Lamb appears,
Promised from eternal years:

> *Hail, thou ever blessed morn;*
> *Hail, redemption's happy dawn;*
> *Sing through all Jerusalem,*
> *Christ is born in Bethlehem.*

Lo, within a manger lies
He who built the starry skies;
He who, throned in height sublime,
Sits amid the cherubim.

Say, ye holy shepherds, say
What your joyful news today;
Wherefore have ye left your sheep
On the lonely mountain steep?

'As we watched at dead of night,
Lo, we saw a wondrous light;
Angels singing, "Peace on Earth",
Told us of our Saviour's birth.'

Teach, O teach us, holy Child,
By thy face so meek and mild,
Teach us to resemble thee,
In thy sweet humility.

Christians, awake

Christians, awake, salute the happy morn,
Whereon the Saviour of the World was born;
Rise to adore the mystery of love,
Which hosts of angels chanted from above;
With them the joyful tidings first begun
Of God incarnate and the Virgin's Son.

Then to the watchful shepherds it was told,
Who heard the angelic herald's voice, 'Behold,
I bring good tidings of a Saviour's birth
To you and all the nations upon Earth;
This day hath God fulfilled his promised word,
This day is born a Saviour, Christ the Lord.'

He spake; and straightway the celestial choir
In hymns of joy, unknown before, conspire.
The praises of redeeming love they sang,
And heaven's whole orb with alleluyas rang:
God's highest glory was their anthem still,
Peace upon Earth, and unto men good will.

To Bethlehem straight the enlightened
    shepherds ran,
To see the wonder God had wrought for man.
He that was born upon this joyful day
Around us all his glory shall display:
Saved by his love, incessant we shall sing
Eternal praise to heaven's almighty King.

God rest you merry gentlemen

God rest you merry gentlemen,
Let nothing you dismay,
For Jesus Christ our Saviour
Was born upon this day,
To save us all from Satan's power
When we were gone astray:
O tidings of comfort and joy,
comfort and joy,
O tidings of comfort and joy.

From God our heavenly Father
A blessed angel came,
And unto certain shepherds
Brought tidings of the same,
How that in Bethlehem was born
The Son of God by name.

The shepherds at those tidings
Rejoiced much in mind,
And left their flocks a-feeding,
In tempest, storm and wind,
And went straightway to Bethlehem
The blessed babe to find.

But when to Bethlehem they came,
Whereat this infant lay,
They found him in a manger,
Where oxen fed on hay;
His mother Mary kneeling,
Unto the Lord did pray.

Now to the Lord sing praises,
All you within this place,
And with true love and brotherhood
Each other now embrace;
This holy tide of Christmas
All other doth deface.

Good King Wenceslas

Good King Wenceslas looked out,
On the Feast of Stephen,
When the snow lay round about,
Deep, and crisp, and even:
Brightly shone the moon that night,
Though the frost was cruel,
When a poor man came in sight,
Gath'ring winter fuel.

'Hither, page, and stand by me,
If thou know'st it, telling.
Yonder peasant, who is he?
Where and what his dwelling?'
'Sire, he lives a good league hence,
Underneath the mountain,
Right against the forest fence,
By Saint Agnes' fountain.'

'Bring me flesh, and bring me wine.
Bring me pine-logs hither:
Thou and I will see him dine,
When we bear them thither.'
Page and monarch, forth they went,
Forth they went together:
Through the rude wind's wild lament
And the bitter weather.

'Sire, the night is darker now,
And the wind blows stronger:
Fails my heart, I know not how;
I can go no longer.'
'Mark my footsteps, good my page;
Tread thou in them boldly:
Thou shalt find the winter's rage
Freeze thy blood less coldly.'

In his master's steps he trod,
Where the snow lay dinted;
Heat was in the very sod
Which the saint had printed.
Therefore, Christian men, be sure,
Wealth or rank possessing,
Ye who now will bless the poor,
Shall yourselves find blessing.

Good Christian men rejoice

Good Christian men, rejoice
With heart and soul and voice!
Give ye heed to what we say:
News! News!
Jesus Christ is born today.
Ox and ass before Him bow,
And He is in the manger now:
Christ is born today.

Good Christian men, rejoice
With heart and soul and voice!
Now ye hear of endless bliss:
Joy! Joy!
Jesus Christ was born for this.
He hath opened the heavenly door,
And man is blest for evermore.
Christ was born for this.

Good Christian men, rejoice
With heart and soul and voice!
Now ye need not fear the grave:
Peace! Peace!
Jesus Christ was born to save;
Calls you one, and calls you all,
To gain His everlasting hall.
Christ was born to save.

Silent night

Silent night! Holy night!
All is calm, all is bright.
Round yon Virgin Mother and Child!
Holy Infant, so tender and mild,
Sleep in heavenly peace!
Sleep in heavenly peace!

Silent night! Holy night!
Shepherds quake at the sight!
Glories stream from heaven afar,
Heavenly hosts sing, "Alleluya!"
Christ, the Saviour, is born!
Christ, the Saviour, is born!

Silent night! Holy night!
Son of God, love's pure light!
Radiant beams from Thy holy face
With the dawn of redeeming grace,
Jesus, Lord, at Thy birth!
Jesus, Lord, at Thy birth!

Unto us a child is born

Unto us a child is born!
King of all creation,
Came he to a world forlorn,
The Lord of every nation.

Cradled in a stall was he
With sleepy cows and asses;
But the very beasts could see
That he all men surpasses.

Herod then with fear was filled:
'A prince,' he said, 'in Jewry!'
All the little boys he killed
At Bethlehem in his fury.

Now may Mary's son, who came
So long ago to love us,
Lead us all with hearts aflame
Unto the joys above us.

Omega and Alpha he!
Let the organ thunder,
While the choir with peals of glee
Doth rend the air asunder.

I saw three ships

I saw three ships come sailing in,
On Christmas Day, on Christmas Day,
I saw three ships come sailing in,
On Christmas Day in the morning.

And what was in those ships all three?
On Christmas Day, on Christmas Day,
And what was in those ships all three?
On Christmas Day in the morning.

'Twas Joseph and his Fair Ladye,
On Christmas Day, on Christmas Day,
'Twas Joseph and his Fair Ladye,
On Christmas Day in the morning.

O, he did whistle and she did sing,
On Christmas Day, on Christmas Day,
O, he did whistle and she did sing,
On Christmas Day in the morning.

Saint Michael was the steeres-man,
On Christmas Day, on Christmas Day,
Saint Michael was the steeres-man,
On Christmas Day in the morning.

Pray, whither sailed those ships all three?
On Christmas Day, on Christmas Day,
Pray, whither sailed those ships all three?
On Christmas Day in the morning.

O, they sailed into Bethlehem,
On Christmas Day, on Christmas Day,
O, they sailed into Bethlehem,
On Christmas Day in the morning.

And all the bells on Earth shall ring,
On Christmas Day, on Christmas Day,
And all the bells on Earth shall ring.
On Christmas Day in the morning.

Ding dong! merrily on high

Ding dong! merrily on high
The bells are gaily ringing;
Ding dong! happily reply
The angels all are singing.
Gloria Hosanna in excelsis.

Ding dong! carol all the bells.
Awake now, do not tarry!
Sing out, sound the good Nowells,
Jesu is born of Mary.
Gloria Hosanna in excelsis.

Ring out, merry merry bells,
The angels all are singing.
Ding dong! swing the steeple bells,
Sound joyous news we're bringing!
Gloria Hosanna in excelsis.

Hark now! happily we sing,
The angels wish us merry!
Ding dong! dancing as we bring
Good news from Virgin Mary.
Gloria Hosanna in excelsis.

As with gladness men of old

As with gladness men of old
Did the guiding star behold,
As with joy they hailed its light,
Leading onward, beaming bright,
So, most gracious Lord, may we
Evermore be led to Thee.

As with joyful steps they sped,
Saviour, to Thy lowly bed,
There to bend the knee before
Thee, whom Heaven and Earth adore,
So may we with willing feet
Ever seek thy mercy-seat.

As they offered gifts most rare
At Thy cradle rude and bare,
So may we with holy joy,
Pure, and free from sin's alloy,
All our costliest treasures bring,
Christ, to Thee, our heavenly King.

Holy Jesus, every day
Keep us in the narrow way;
And, when earthly things are past,
Bring our ransomed souls at last
Where they need no star to guide,
Where no clouds Thy glory hide.

In the heavenly country bright
Need they no created light;
Thou its light, its joy, its crown,
Thou its sun which goes not down;
There for ever may we sing
Hallelujahs to our King.